If I Was Yo' Daddy

Curated By

T.Stone

DEDICATION

I dedicate this book to Zavier, Dimitri, & Sadie - and to all the young Kings and Queens of the world. Never stop imagining, never stop learning., & never stop believing in your dreams. YOU ARE THE FUTURE!

ACKNOWLEDGMENTS

I would like to thank Brooke Yates and all the men that gave their advice whole heartedly, your participation helped make this book possible. You are all Kings and it must be noted! Black men are Kings. It must be noted! -Blessings

A Collection of Life Advice from Black Kings...

Preface...

Society has many factors that are disruptive to the learning, growth, and overall experience of our youth. Factors such as lack of self-knowledge, poverty, absent parents, learning disabilities, and or limited opportunities and motivation. This book consists of advice from those that have not only encountered these experiences, but have overcome them in some form. The question presented to them was "If you could tell your child or the 'younger you' anything what would it be?"

If I could tell my younger self something I would say...

"One thing that I would tell myself if I could go back in time, is to "Make Every Day Count." Whatever dream you have that you "think" is out of reach or you "feel" is too hard for you, CAN be accomplished!! Nothing in life will come free, you have to work hard for what you want, because nothing is going to be handed to you. Keep God first and love with a pure heart" -"That's really the main thing". - Anonymous King

If I could tell my younger self something I would say...

"Don't make decisions that will result in a felony"

- Anonymous King

"You can alter your whole life with the smallest change." - *Anonymous King*

If I was Yo' Daddy, I would tell you...

"Respect your parents and always stand up for yourself. Never let anyone bring you down, no one is that powerful. And again, respect your parents always! They might yell at you or get mad at you, but the reason so is because they want you to succeed in life. And their goal is to make sure you're better than them. -Anonymous King

If I was Yo' Daddy, I would tell you...

Always be true to yourself don't allow people to control who you are, and in every decision always consider the outcome of any choice" - Anonymous King

"Never lose the identity of who you are"...- Anonymous King

If I was Yo' Daddy, I would tell you...

"Always trust your instincts and never be afraid of following them." - Anonymous King

"Stay true to who you are even if people don't like it." - Anonymous King

If I could tell my younger self something I would say...

"You are judged by your character not by your costume." - Anonymous King

"Hone into your powers from God that's the only way". - Anonymous King

If I could tell my younger self something I would say...

"The material things in life do not matter and will eventually fade away, but time is your most valuable possession. You can replace a lot of things in life, but you cannot replace time- so save your money and keep your family first and most importantly keep God with you at all times." - Anonymous King

If I was Yo' daddy, I would tell you...

"Stick to your gut feeling. Everyone isn't meant to understand what you do or
have to like what you do, as long as it brings you happiness and doesn't harm anyone or anything's well- being, do it!!" - Anonymous King

"Always be a leader and go after the things you

desire." - Anonymous King

If I was Yo' Daddy, I would tell you...

"Always look a man in the eye when you shake his hand." - Anonymous King

"Have integrity at all times." - Anonymous King

"If you give your word keep it!" - Anonymous King

If I could tell my younger self anything I would say...

"Everything is an illusion. "- Anonymous King

If I was Yo' Daddy, I would tell you...

"Word is bond!"- Anonymous King

"Work for yourself ONLY!" - Anonymous King

If I was Yo' Daddy, I would tell you...

"Work on spirituality not religion." - Anonymous King

"Dream Big"- Anonymous King

If I was Yo' Daddy, I would tell you...

"Live!" - Anonymous King

If I could tell my younger self something I would say...

"No one will give you what you want you have to work hard for it every day!" - Anonymous King

"Trust in God."- Anonymous King

If I was Yo' Daddy, I would tell you...

"Stay true to yourself." - Anonymous King

"Leap for your dreams even when it seems tough!" - Anonymous King

"Take calculated risks and never waste time on things you're not in love with."- Anonymous King

"No one can tell you what you can't do." - Anonymous King

If I was Yo' Daddy, I would tell you...

"Never try to prove people wrong, when you follow your dreams your success will prove you right." - Anonymous King

"You have the power to create from a thought which is the beginning to something tangible." - Anonymous King

If I was Yo' Daddy, I would tell you...

"Never stop recognizing what this world needs." - Anonymous King

"Bless this world with actions inspired by deep thought." - Anonymous King

"Never give up on your dreams and aspirations." - Anonymous King

If I could tell my younger self something I would say...

"Life is a marathon not a race; you have no control of it, but instead participate in it, so decide the position you want to be in!" - Anonymous King

If I could tell my younger self something I would say...

"Always practice on controlling your emotions." - Anonymous King

"Think before you speak." - Anonymous King

If I was Yo' Daddy, I would tell you...

"Never underestimate the value of respect." - Anonymous King

"Respect creates honor, honor shows loyalty, loyalty leads to greatness!"- Anonymous King

"If you can dream it, you can make it your reality!" - Anonymous King

If I was Yo' Daddy, I would tell you...

"Nothing in life is really a loss, instead it's all about how you look at it."- Anonymous King

"In life every negative can be turned into a positive depending on your perception of it." - Anonymous King

If I could tell my younger self something I would say...

"Be yourself, it lasts longer" - Anonymous King

"Stay away from the streets!!" - Anonymous King

If I could tell my younger self something I would say...

"Your mind is the greatest battle you will ever have to face. If you win the battle in your mind and constantly train it the same way most do their bodies, you can conquer anything that comes your way." - Anonymous King

If I was Yo' Daddy, I would tell you...

"Don't be a follower be a leader and always follow your first mind" - Anonymous King

If I was Yo' Daddy, I would tell you...

"Always be a positive thinker, because positive energy breeds positive results"- Anonymous King

If I could tell my younger self something I would say...

"Life has no rules. Everything is made up. If you decide to drop out of school make sure to develop a plan of what you are going to do after and do it immediately, it's not worth your time suffering and letting your creative potential fade." -

Anonymous King

If I was Yo' Daddy, I would tell you...

"Stay in school, stay focused, never disrespect your elders, don't let anyone influence you to do something that will alter your life, having you dead or in jail." - Anonymous King

"You are a black king not a nigga". - Anonymous King

If I could tell my younger self something I would say...

"Nobody is going to come save you so save yourself! Learn how to focus your energy and meditate on what you want for your life -speak it and watch it come into fruition. Stand firm on what you believe and remember you are the God of your own destiny!" - Anonymous King

"Just be patient"...- Anonymous King

"Stand Up for Yourself, believe in yourself, and love yourself!" - Anonymous King

If I was Yo' Daddy, I would tell you...

"Son.... forget not my law...and keep the Almighty's commandments." - Anonymous King

If I could tell my younger self something I would say...

"The penitentiary was created for men that makes impulsive decisions based on their feelings. Always be in control of your environment by conducting yourself to be set apart from the average; And always be opposite of statistical views that classifies you in a specific category."- Anonymous King

If I was Yo' Daddy, I would tell you...

"Love yourself and never give up." - Anonymous

King

If I could tell my younger self something I would say...

"Learn proper communication skills and build people up with positivity."- Anonymous King

" If you don't stand for something you will fall for anything." - Anonymous King

"Do what truly make you happy and don't follow trends." - Anonymous King

If I was Yo' Daddy, I would tell you...

"Don't stress over what you cannot control. Stay focused on your goals, be true to yourself, educate yourself in all aspects, and be patient- everything comes with time." - Anonymous King

"As a man thinketh so he is,
Elevation is a constant struggle, and circumstances don't mold you, they only reveal to you who you really are." - Anonymous King

If I was Yo' Daddy, I would tell you...

"Never be a people pleaser."- Anonymous King

"You have to sacrifice and learn. Life is hard and things will happen." - Anonymous King

If I could tell my younger self something I would say...

"Do what truly makes you happy because no one has to live your life but YOU!!"- Anonymous King

If I was Yo' Daddy, I would tell you...

"Never turn your back on those who were always there for you!" - Anonymous King

"If your heart is not in it, get out of it!!"-
Anonymous King

If I was Yo' Daddy, I would tell you...

"Remember to call your parents." - Anonymous
King

"You live, you learn, but you learn to live." -
Anonymous King

"I would most definitely tell my son "anything
you want in life GO FOR IT". "Never let a
person convince you that you're not capable or
qualified to do anything. Ambition is the key to

success" - Anonymous King

"Focus on school not on sex... It will always be there." - Anonymous King

If I could tell my younger self something I would say...

"Chase your dreams and don't let anyone get in the way of your path.
While you're chasing your dreams you will get to a point where it will get really scary, that's the part where you see how strong you are.
Face all your fears!!" - Anonymous King

"Life is not about how many times you fall, but instead how many times you get up." - Anonymous King

"If I could tell my younger self anything it would be to always believe in yourself, never stop having faith regardless of what is going on, because the power of BELIEVING is real!" - Anonymous King

If I could tell my younger self something I would say...

"Have patience, don't rush to do things out of desperation. Good credit is golden, and also spend more time with family because the people you call friends are not your friend. Don't ever feel sorry for yourself; keep pushing - a failure is just a stepping stone for your come up." - Anonymous

King

"Tomorrow is not promised, but tomorrow will come." - Anonymous King

If I could tell my younger self something I would say...

"Never settle, and don't give up until you go up." - Anonymous King

"Trust your instincts and never be afraid of following them." - Anonymous King

If I could tell my younger self something I would say...

"Save money, be selective with women, travel

even more and do whatever comes to mind now, because time is not forever. Dubai will not be the same type of fun at 60 as it is at 25 so go now!"- Anonymous King

"I wasted a lot of time chasing girls and I got most of them. I thought it would satisfy or complete me in some way, but it didn't. I realize now it was my ego, and I really was just spreading myself thin, which would later lead to lots of mental pain and self -hatred. After over 150 female partners I would say not to validate yourself by women or money. Love yourself and realize that when you give and show the world who you are you will have all the love and friends you need." - Anonymous King

"What I have learned from my experience in life is that you can't do anything without God, and it's nothing you can't do with him in your corner! "Strive for greatness against all odds and let your mistakes be your success." - Anonymous King

If I could tell my younger self something I would tell me...

" Think about all the worst outcomes before you decide to do anything! - Rather good or bad... - Anonymous King

"Once you put your mind to something, make it happen, the road is going to get bumpy, but as long as you stay focused on the big picture the mission will be a successful one. Never follow behind parked cars!" -Anonymous King

If I could tell my younger self something I would tell me...

"Learn to live life in accordance to respect. Respect is essentially the determining factor of how high you go in life. Even though it is earned and not given, you must give respect to get it, walk with respect in a dignified way, talk with respect to each person, especially queens of all kind. Respect the elders for they can give examples of life lessons that you may not currently understand. Respect those younger than you, for they may not know the way of respect taught in a way that was taught to you. Respect life and live it the best way you can legitimately live!" - Anonymous King

"Believe in yourself! Never allow anyone to place

their limitations on you." - Anonymous King

"A wise man learns from others' mistakes while a fool learns from his own." - Anonymous King

"Be your own cheerleader.

Be your own supporter.

Be your biggest fan.

Speak life over yourself!" - Anonymous King

If I was Yo' Daddy, I would tell you...

"Sometimes we have to truly see the gifts and talents we've been blessed to carry...A lot of times people don't see it and that's cool. You know what you carry and you don't need the validation & confirmation, of anyone. Walk that thing out and see how far you go when you believe in yourself. " - Anonymous King

"Be the *best* version of yourself &
never let anyone stop you from pursuing your
dreams...Keep God first." -Anonymous King

If I was Yo' Daddy, I would tell you...

"Don't let nothing or nobody tell you who you are
or try to stop you from being what you want to be.
Always strive for greatness. The sky is not the
limit it goes way beyond!" - Anonymous King

"Keep your mind on your dreams. Don't let
nothing or nobody tell you what you can and
cannot do. Always strive for greatness." -
Anonymous King

If I could tell my younger self something it would be...

"If I can't love them the way they need to be loved, don't waste their time. I have hurt a lot of people in my past by not being fully aware of who I was as a person, and not being emotionally mature enough to let some people go so that they could receive the love they gave to me in return."

"If I could tell the younger me one thing it would be that it's ok that you're growing up without a father. Friends can't replace that and it's ok to be alone." - Anonymous King

Be patient, nothing happens overnight, don't ever give up. When things look bad that's just a test from God, so keep it moving because it's always another day - Anonymous King

"There is no Success without Successors"

The African proverbial phrase, "It takes a village to raise a child", is certainly applicable at levels of our life, and is not limited to young children, teens, or young adolescents and is by no means exclusive to a specific gender, class, or ethnic group. It originated from the Nigerian Igbo culture and proverb "Ora na azu nwa," which means it takes the community/village to raise a child. The Igbo's also name their children "Nwa ora" which means child of the community. But let's face it, we are all challenged to maintain our competitive edge in an ever-evolving cultural and socio-economic world that places strong demands on its human capital outlay. It is also very glaring that our village has long since been expanded beyond the reach of our neighboring domiciles.

We no longer live in silos bounded by geographical limitations. In fact, we live in a global economy much like a global village, and the world is our community, wherein each member affects the lives of the populous at-large. As Dr. King recited to the graduating class of Springfield College on June 14, 1964, just 10 months after the *I Have a Dream* speech and six months before receiving the Nobel Peace Prize, "we are caught in an inescapable network of mutuality, tied in a single garment of destiny. Whatever affects one directly, affects all indirectly, for injustice anywhere is a threat to justice everywhere!"

Much like Dr. King, I definitely learned a lot from my mom and dad, but I learned equally from the people in my circles, and those who were not. Adaptation is a fundamental human trait that has a direct and indirect impact on our lives. Momma used to say, "Watch who you hang around and one who hangs around you." It is critical that we are cognizant of the power of influence. We inevitably have either positive or negative influences on everyone we directly or indirectly encounter. As the potter shapes the clay, our life's encounters shape our behavior, thoughts, feelings, attitude, and actions.

Referring back to the African proverb, where it takes a village to raise a child...I challenge you to the two quintessential underlying questions that oftentimes remain stealth in the mindset of so many people who embrace this historical philosophy. These two questions are established on the premise, if it takes a village to raise a child then who trains the village and who in the village is invited to the training because human progress does not roll on the wheels of inevitability. If we want to attain true progress, we must continue to teach-one-to-reach-one or as many as we can, one day at a time. To all the readers, be mindful that we learn something best when we teach it to others and at the end of the day, Pastor Munroe Myles said it best, there is no success without successors. #getatit! -Anonymous King

IF I WAS YO' MAMA....

I would tell you to find your "TOPS"... TALENTS, OPPORTUNITIES, PASSION, and SKILLS. Identify them and cultivate them. What you are talented in you may not necessarily find opportunity in, what you're passionate about you may have to learn certain skills to pursue, what you have skills in may not be what you want to do, but that's ok. Identify your TOPS and hone in on your craft, that way, you can take the money you make from your skills and invest it in your passions, which can create your own opportunity with your talents. Don't wait on opportunities, create them! Humans are born to create, so never allow anyone to tell you that you're too young to accomplish your dreams.

You got this! Everything you need is already in you. RNA turns into DNA so our ancestors' knowledge is always with us. You are here for a purpose. Enjoy your life and leave your imprint on the world so deep that generations after you will still feel and see it! Remember you're never too old to learn or too young to teach! Be blessed... Keep God first... Learn yourself... Learn the laws and principles of the Universe and you will see how much they relate to your life. Everything is an emulation of the brain or body of a human. Never stop paying attention and never stop asking questions or finding solutions. Everything is cause and effect so make sure your actions are always aligned with good intent. Be the light that God intended you to be. - T. Stone

Behind the veil lies your true self

ABOUT THE AUTHORS

T. resides in Houston, Texas and is originally from Linden, Alabama. Focusing on books and film, her goal is to produce content that reinforce growth, development, communion, liberation, and expression within the black community. She is a writer, entrepreneur, poet, and educator. She obtained her B.A in Radio Television Film & M.A in Professional Communications from Texas Southern University.

I hope this book reach you with love and light. -T. Stone

www.ingramcontent.com/pod-product-compliance
Lightning Source LLC
Chambersburg PA
CBHW060943050426
42453CB00009B/1112